REPORT ON

HM YOUNG OFFENDER INSTITUTION

AYLESBURY

BY

HM CHIEF INSPECTOR OF PRISONS

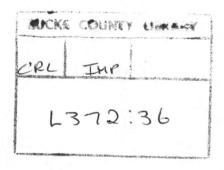

Crown Copyright 1992
Printed in England
by the Home Office, London

ISBN 0 86252 840 2
Published by
Home Office
50 Queen Anne's Gate
London SW1H 9AT

PREFACE

1. A specific problem at Aylesbury is of urgent concern. It became clear to our Inspectors that the establishment was inadequately secure for Category A inmates, in particular because of proximity of buildings to the perimeter wall and the ensuing impossibility of an appropriate inner wall, and because of certain difficulties with the current gate, which is not due for replacement for several years. Following a statement of our findings, the Prison Service at a very high level arranged for the movement out of six Category A inmates. Three of them were transferred appropriately to adult status. The other three are younger, and have been transferred to the segregation unit at Gartree and thence to a unit at Albany. Neither of these adult prisons can provide a suitable regime for them. More Category A Young Offenders are due soon to be sent to Aylesbury, which for some time has been treated as the centre for them.

2. Castington and Swinfen Hall and Aylesbury are the three establishments used for long-term Young Offenders generally. They are not convenient for family visits for the great majority of the inmates, and their locations certainly do not accord with the community prison principles of the Woolf Report and the Government's White Paper.

3. Two questions are raised:

    (a) What should happen to the three inmates now in Albany and others destined in the near future for Aylesbury?

(b) What should be the role for Aylesbury in the future for Category A Young Offenders?

4. As to the first question, it must be for line management rather than for an inspection report. I do not advise on individual cases. I comment only that it may be possible to hold such offenders temporarily in Aylesbury, on a basis of containing them in the main prison rather than on F or G Wings, of providing them with occupation such as education, gym and wing cleaning (but not the Braille work). They would not be able to get open air exercise. I make no recommendation, but leave the proposal to be considered.

5. What should be the future role for Aylesbury in relation to Category A? The Estate Review for 1991 does not deal with the question or with the future of Aylesbury at all. Can Aylesbury be sufficiently secure to hold Category A Young Offenders in the future, or should somewhere else be chosen? A very large sum of money has recently been spent on making the cells and accommodation secure. It might be possible either to secure the perimeter, or else to create a secure unit inside. Unless one or other of these courses can be and is followed, clearly Category A Young Offenders will have to go elsewhere. It is not at all obvious where they should go.

6. Where are these decisions made? Are they to be reached by the Area Manager and his Operational Director, or are they to be reached in DOC 1, its Category A unit or its Director? Are they to be reached by even higher authority? The uncertainty

points to a weakness of organisation which needs to be addressed. I can do no more than raise the urgent issues.

Stephen Tumim
HM Chief Inspector of Prisons

INTRODUCTION

This is one of a series of reports produced by HM Inspectorate of Prisons and presented to the Home Secretary about the treatment of inmates and the conditions in Prison Service establishments in England and Wales.

The inspection of Aylesbury Young Offender Institution took place from 8 to 12 July 1991.

Recommendations of a minor cr housekeeping nature have been referred directly to the Governor (and copied to Prison Service Headquarters). They are not included in Chapter Eight of this Report. By arrangement, a member of the Health and Safety Section of the Home Office visited Aylesbury whilst we were there and our comments and recommendations about health and safety matters were informed by his advice and expertise for which we are grateful.

HM Inspectorate publishes an Annual Report which explains its method of operation and draws more general conclusions about the work of the Prison Service. Appendix 1 of the report of the Chief Inspector of Prisons 1982 (HC260 published by HMSO) set out the terms of reference of the Inspectorate.

Home Office
September 1991

CONTENTS

		Paragraph	Page
PREFACE			1
INTRODUCTION			5
CHAPTER ONE	**BACKGROUND**		
Section A	**The Establishment**		
	History and role	1.01-1.02	11
	Site	1.03-1.05	11
	Buildings	1.06-1.10	12
	Maintenance	1.11-1.14	13
	Works Services Department	1.15	14
	Development	1.16	15
	Security	1.17	15
	Health and Safety	1.18-1.20	16
	Fire precautions	1.21-1.23	16
	Facilities for people with disabilities	1.24	17
Section B	**The Board of Visitors**	1.25-1.28	17
CHAPTER TWO	**MANAGEMENT, COMMUNICATIONS AND STAFF**		
Section A	**Management**		
	Management structure	2.01-2.04	19
	Operational cover	2.05-2.06	20
	Management Services	2.07-2.12	21
	Information technology	2.13	22
	Equal opportunities	2.14	23
Section B	**Communications**		
	Meetings	2.15-2.24	23
	Industrial relations	2.25-2.26	25
Section C	**Staffing**		
	Staff facilities	2.27-2.28	26
	Staff perceptions	2.29-2.32	27
	Staff complement and deployment	2.33-2.35	28
	Staff training	2.36-2.38	29

		Paragraph	Page
CHAPTER THREE	**INMATES**		
Section A	**The inmate population**		
	Inmate profile and catchment area	3.01-3.04	30
	Inmate perceptions	3.05	31
	Race Relations	3.06-3.11	33
Section B	**Settling-in**		
	Reception	3.12-3.14	34
	Induction and information to inmates	3.15-3.17	35
	Sentence calculation	3.18	36
	Allocation to accommodation	3.19-3.20	37
	Inmate accommodation	3.21-3.24	37
	Inmate facilities	3.25-3.28	38
Section C	**Discipline and control**		
	Good order	3.29-3.33	39
	Segregation Unit	3.34-3.38	40
	Adjudications	3.39-3.42	42
	Escape list	3.43	43
	Closed Visits	3.44	43
	Searching	3.45-3.46	44
	Drugs	3.47	44
CHAPTER FOUR	**REGIME**		
Section A	**Routines**		
	Association	4.01-4.02	45
	Exercise	4.03	45
	Meal times	4.04	46
Section B	**Services**		
	Pay and private cash	4.05	46
	Shop	4.06-4.08	47
	Clothing and Kit	4.09-4.10	48
	Catering	4.11-4.13	49
	Legal aid and appeals	4.14	50
	Privileges	4.15	50
	Requests and complaints procedures	4.16-4.17	51
Section C	**Activities**		
	Employment	4.18-4.20	52
	Farms and Gardens	4.21	53
	Education	4.22-4.25	53

		Paragraph	Page
	Vocational Training Courses	4.26-4.27	55
	Construction Industry		
	Training Courses	4.28-4.29	56
	Library	4.30-4.31	56
	Physical Education	4.32-4.33	57
	Religious activities	4.34-4.37	57
	Community activities	4.38	58
	Regime monitoring	4.39	59

CHAPTER FIVE   **RESETTLEMENT**

Section A   **Family Links**

	Visits	5.01-5.02	60
	Letters and telephones	5.03-5.04	61
	Prison Visitors	5.05	61

Section B   **Throughcare**

	Personal Officer scheme and		
	review procedures	5.06	62
	Probation	5.07-5.12	62
	Psychological Services		
	Department	5.13-5.16	64
	Local Review Committee	5.17-5.18	66
	Recategorisation and transfer	5.19	66
	Temporary release	5.20	67
	Pre-release	5.21	67

CHAPTER SIX   **MEDICAL AND SPECIAL FEATURES**

Section A   **Medical Services**

	Staffing	6.01-6.03	68
	The Hospital	6.04-6.07	69
	Pharmacy	6.08	70
	Dental services	6.09-6.10	70
	Psychiatric services	6.11	71
	Injuries and self-inflicted	6.12-6.13	71
	harm		
	Sexually-transmitted diseases	6.14	72

Section B   **Special Features**

	Lifers	6.15-6.18	72

CHAPTER SEVEN   **CONCLUSIONS**   7.01-7.08   74

		Paragraph	Page
CHAPTER EIGHT	**RECOMMENDATIONS**		
	Director General	8.01-8.14	77
	Governor	8.15-8.102	79

APPENDICES

		Page
1.	Breakdown of population by sentence length	89
2.	Management structure	91
3.	Employment profile	93
4.	Policy statement - Race and Equal Opportunities	95
5.	Aylesbury's Statement of Purpose	97
6.	PE Programme	99
7.	Inspection team	101

CHAPTER ONE

BACKGROUND

Section A   The Establishment

History and role

1.01   Aylesbury has had a gaol for many centuries.
The present young offender institution, constructed well
outside the town in 1847, was built to hold debtors,
felons and women inmates. Its former inhabitants would
have little difficulty in recognising many of the
buildings today. A centre for inebriate women was added
on land adjoining the prison in 1902; this functioned
independently until 1930 when it was incorporated with
the prison and used as a Borstal for girls, until 1959.
From 1960, the establishment has housed only male
offenders.

1.02   At the time of the inspection, it held mainly
long-term inmates in the 17-20 age bracket. Of the 243
young men detained in the institution on 9 July, 137
were serving sentences of between 4 and 10 years and a
further 36 life sentences. Most of the population was
from London and the South-East. The Governor told us
that the inmates' home addresses covered every county in
England except two. It is in no sense a community
prison.

Site

1.03   The estate comprised the prison itself within a
walled secure perimeter, occupying about nine hectares
of land, together with sundry quarters, the bulk of
which were on an adjoining estate.

1.04   The institution is situated alongside the main Aylesbury to Leighton Buzzard road some two miles from Aylesbury town centre in a pleasant, residential suburb. A small forecourt joins the road to the original Gatehouse and makes access for vehicles easier. Once inside, between the Gate and the main entrance to the prison buildings, there is a very restricted turning area. The different buildings within the perimeter are spaciously laid out and connected by an extensive system of roads and paths, between lawns and flower beds. The most southerly part of the site, furthest from the Gate, is a large, grassed sports field outside the perimeter wall but enclosed by a single five metre wire fence with access via a gateway which breached the perimeter wall (see also 1.17).

1.05   The site slopes substantially away from the Gatehouse; the ground is stable and well-drained. Mains water, gas, drainage and electricity are all connected; there is a fully automatic, standby diesel generator capable of accepting the connected load. The large, central steam boiler plant, which once serviced the site, has recently been replaced by small, individual gas-fired boilers.

Buildings

1.06   The buildings fall into three age groups: the original ones from 1847, those added in 1902 and later infill additions.

1.07   The 1847 buildings comprise (in addition to the original perimeter wall) the two-storey Gatehouse, a three-storey, three main wing radial prison block with an additional, ancillary department wing and single-storey out buildings. They are in the classical Victorian-Georgian prison style in a red local brick with sandstone quoins and decorations. Walls are solid;

12

floors are also solid but with some timber in limited areas. Roofs are pitched on timber trusses, the original slate covering having been replaced by man-made slate of almost identical appearance.

1.08   The 1902 group comprises two, three-storey residential blocks, a three-storey office block and some ancillary accommodation. The residential blocks have a nondescript architectural style. Construction is in a similar red brick to that of the older buildings but with the added embellishment of yellow brick stringer courses running the length of the structures by way of decoration. Floors are solid; roofs are pitched, again with the original slate replaced by the man-made variety matching the other blocks.

1.09   The infill buildings are in mixed styles and constructions ranging from modern, two and single-storey red brick blocks to the concrete slab and slotted post type so common in agriculture. Roof coverings vary from asbestos based cement sheeting to flat roofs to modern pre-formed metal sheeting. All floors are solid.

1.10   A considerable run of new perimeter walling has been added to the original section. It is in concrete but clad internally and externally with red bricks to match existing structures. Additionally, the original wall has been strengthened by external piers in the same modern red brick.

Maintenance
1.11   The buildings and estate are in very good physical condition with only a small number of predictable minor defects. These have been identified in the secondary recommendations we make directly to the Governor (and which are not listed in this report).

1.12   Internally, the buildings had unwashed walls, unswept floors and accumulations of dirt in all but the most easily accessible places. The recesses were not properly cleaned with WCs slop sinks and urinals heavily lime scaled. Exceptions, where minimum cleaning standards were achieved, were the Contract Services Workshop (where the copper pipes were polished) the Braille Workshop (commendably clean) and the inmates' own cells.

1.13   The decoration appeared generally to be good but the layers of dirt in places made assessment of conditions difficult. The wings were mostly decorated in light colours which could be adopted elsewhere to replace the prevalent 'government buff'.

1.14   The grounds were generally free from accumulated rubbish except for the rear of G Wing. Recent demolitions, and the imminent onset of more building work, had left the grounds untidy and many of the flower beds and lawns showed signs of serious neglect (see also paragraph 4.21). Floor finishes were in a particularly poor condition, especially where modern tiles had been laid over the original quarry tiles and were now coming loose over wide areas. We noted that some staff were not using the Small Repairs System to report minor repairs; all staff should be encouraged to do so.

Works Services Department
1.15   The Works Services Department was headed by a Governor 4 (Works) who had three Principal Officers (Works) working to him. The Department was well housed in new, but inconveniently sited accommodation. It was located outside the perimeter wall at the back of the prison with access via the main Gate. Administration of the department was generally good and it appeared

adequately staffed for the workload. There was a
forward programme of work which will maintain the value
of the estate.

Development

1.16   Major works for the financial year 1990-91
included a new water main and drainage for the site and
the first phase of the integral sanitation programme;
this was to be in G Wing which would be extensively
refurbished and upgraded at the same time. We
understood that similar work in A Wing would be unlikely
to start before 1994/95. Other projects included the
provision of a secondary fence to the sports field -
awaiting confirmation of funding - and the new Gate
complex (including new reception and visiting
facilities), work was scheduled to begin in 1992-93. It
was disappointing to learn that a Visitor's Centre was
unlikely to be included in the project. Finally, a new
hospital complex was due to be built but this would take
four years to complete from whenever the design brief
was settled. We comment on some of these development
projects in other parts of the report.

Security

1.17   The physical security had a number of weaknesses
which caused us to believe it was not adequate for an
establishment holding Category A inmates. Our concern
leads us to recommend that no Category A inmates (even
those of only standard escape potential) should be
allocated to the institution until security has been
improved to appropriate Category A standards. We have
made a number of more detailed comments and
recommendations about security directly to the Secretary
of State; in the interests of security, they are not
published in this report. We draw attention to the
issues raised in the Preface.

Health and Safety

1.18   The Health and Safety Committee was well constituted, met regularly and its meetings were adequately minuted. The Accident Reporting System was in place and working.

1.19   The Health and Safety Policy and Statement of Arrangements document was wrongly titled and not easy to follow; it should be amplified and clarified. Safety Audits lacked direction and were behind schedule; they should be programmed and brought up-to-date. Work on the Control of Substances Hazardous to Health Regulations was seriously behind and should receive prompt attention. The Safe Methods of Working documents were incomplete; they should be completed for the whole establishment.

1.20   We noted that not all cold rooms had permanently-lit, internal lights and labels on door release catches. We also noted that the victualling cold store should have an alarm, an insulated door and door catch release; deficiencies should be remedied. We have made a further number of minor health and safety recommendations directly to the Governor and these are not included as part of this report.

Fire precautions

1.21   The duties of Fire Officer were primarily the responsibility of one Officer who had received appropriate training. He was supported by a deputy who was still awaiting an opportunity to attend a training course. We thought that more officers needed to be familiar with at least the basic routines of the Fire Officer to ensure more expertise was regularly available.

1.22   There was not a proper allocation of hours for
the Fire Officer to complete his full range of duties.
In the time available, it was not possible to check
equipment as required. The workload of the Fire Officer
should be reviewed so that the appropriate amount of
time can be allocated for the completion of the various
tasks.

1.23   An evacuation fire drill had recently been
carried out and had gone well. Fire exit routes needed
to be more clearly marked. Liaison with the local Fire
Service was said to be excellent with regular
familiarisation visits and tours of the establishment.
Their reaction time for attending an emergency was two
minutes.

Facilities for people with disabilities
1.24   Little, if any thought, had been given to the
needs of disabled inmates or to visitors to the
establishment suffering from any disability. Similarly,
no provision had been made to assist disabled people to
work in the institution. Facilities for the disabled
should therefore be surveyed annually as part of the
Health and Safety audit and appropriate provision made.

Section B   Board of Visitors

1.25   We met the Chairman of the Board of Visitors and
separately the full Board. Membership had fallen from
16 to 12 members. Nominations for vacant posts had been
submitted.

1.26   The Board had neither an office nor a
telephone - reports on visits were typed by members at
home. These facilities should be provided and a typing

service arranged. Members carried keys and had free
access to the establishment at all times. Staff were
described as helpful and supportive.

1.27   Among the concerns raised by the Chairman was
the low number of discipline staff and the high
proportion of junior staff. The difficulties faced by
young staff moving into the area were recognised. The
Board considered there should be increased opportunities
for inmates to work with their hands - for example, on a
bricklaying course or in a motor mower repair shop. The
Personal Officer scheme was working well. The
importance of this scheme was emphasised when members of
the Board paid their weekly visit to the Induction Unit.

1.28   The full Board added two additional concerns.
One was the need to provide appropriate medical cover
and facilities for psychiatrically disturbed inmates and
the second, the need for Prison Service Headquarters to
recognise the unique role of Aylesbury within the Young
Offender system. The future of that unique role may
depend on the resolution of issues raised in the
Preface.

CHAPTER TWO

MANAGEMENT, COMMUNICATIONS AND STAFF

Section A   Management

Management structure

2.01   Aylesbury was managed by a Governor 2 who was accountable to the Area Manager for the Chilterns area. The Governor was supported by six functional heads who reported directly to him as set out in the table below:-

Functional Head	Grade
Custody	Governor 4
Inmate Activities	Governor 4
Works Services	Governor 4
Management Services	Higher Executive Officer
Medical Services	Medical Officer (part-time)
Psychological Services	Principal Psychologist

2.02   The custody function was divided between three Governors 5 and the Senior Probation Officer (SPO). One Governor 5 was responsible for operations and security, another for A, B and C Wings and the Segregation Unit, and the third, for F and G Wings. The SPO was responsible for his department, reporting directly to the Head of Custody. The Head of Inmate Activities was responsible for the work of the Chaplain, the Education Officer, the Industrial Manager, the Principal Officer Physical Education Instructor and the Senior Officer Caterer. We discuss Works Services, Management Services, Psychological and Medical Services elsewhere in the report (see paragraphs 1.15, 2.07, 5.13 and 6.01 respectively).

2.03   The allocation of management responsibilities was sound and in keeping with Fresh Start principles apart from the Custody Office which had remained with the Head of Management Services (HOMS). We have noted an increasing tendency for the linkage between Management Services Departments and Discipline (or Custody) Offices to remain (or be reinstated).

2.04   We concluded that the Governor's style made an important contribution to the way in which the management structure operated. This was typified by the introduction of a more personal and approachable way of managing and a conscious effort to devolve work and decisions to the lowest appropriate level. The latter approach enhanced the status and the work of the staff.

Operational cover

2.05   The Governor normally worked a five-day week. Weekend duties were performed by a Governor 4 and a Governor 5 with any absences covered by the Governor himself or the Head of Works Services.

2.06   The duty Governor system included all the Governor grades apart from the governing Governor. The duty governor was the Operational Commander of the establishment throughout the 24 hour period of the duty. His responsibilities included attending the emergency control room for all incidents (including alarm bells), authorising the planned use of control and restraint procedures, and remaining in the establishment during evening association. We asked about access to emergency orders when the duty Governor was at home and were satisfied with the arrangements. We considered that governor grade cover was properly organised and readily available if required.

Management Services

2.07 The Head of Management Services was a Higher Executive Officer and the following staff reported to her:-

Grade	Number of staff
Executive Officer	2
Personal Secretary	1
Administrative Officer	8[a]
Typist	2[a]
Administrative Assistant	3
Training Principal Officer	1
Prison Auxiliary	2
Storeman	2
Assistant Storeman	1

Note a. 1 part-time

2.08 A freeze on recruitment had adversely affected administrative support to the Education and the Probation Departments. The ban had only added to the view that the staffing of Management Services (MS) was too tight and was inhibiting the Department's full development. There was, in our view, sufficient justification for a resource review and we recommend accordingly. We hope that the outcome would allow MS to be able to provide appropriate administrative support to the Probation and Education Departments. Despite what was seen as inadequate staffing, it was acknowledged that there had been significant movement away from being a pre-Fresh Start Administration Officer's Department. In particular, there was a recognition of the work which MS should undertake in the personnel and staff training fields.

2.09 The responsibility for the Discipline Office remained with the Head of Management Services; sentence

calculation and diary checks were undertaken by a
Governor 5.   There had been a comparatively low number
of inmates received in the year to 31 March 1991 (159).

2.10   Cash checks were carried out regularly by the
HOMS and by the Governor. We were told that the number
of invoices being paid locally was increasing.   There
were difficulties in reconciling the prisoners' monies
account and this had been reported. Inmates spending
from private cash was carefully monitored and
controlled; decisions about individual items were
referred to the Governor.

2.11   There were problems with the control and
exchange of kit.   There had been two abortive attempts
to introduce a personal kit system (see also paragraphs
4.09 and 4.10).   Difficulties existed with the supply of
stores; requests were often only partially met by Supply
and Transport Branch with no substitute items offered.
Victualling worked well and was within the cash limit
giving the best possible value for money.

2.12   The HOMS chaired two committees, Health and
Safety and Staff Training.   Both were regarded by the
HOMS as extending and improving her role, but they also
demanded more time and more specialised knowledge from
the postholder.

Information technology
2.13   The establishment was to be surveyed in August
1991 regarding the planned installation of a local
Inmate Database System (LIDS) scheduled for
November/December 1991.   There was a clear recognition
of the various demands that would result.   These
included the need to appoint appropriate database
administrators and to ensure that the transition from
manual to computerised working was smooth and efficient.

Enthusiasm for the new technology was tempered only by apprehension of the demands it would make on what were already considered to be over-worked staff.

Equal opportunities

2.14   Aylesbury operated a policy of equal opportunities and had published a local policy statement (reproduced at Appendix 4). This was to be supplemented by a local grievance procedure which was being discussed with staff association representatives.

Section B   Communications

Meetings

2.15   In April 1991, the Governor had published a notice to staff which announced a revised timetable of meetings. The notice also emphasised that decisions were to be taken at the lowest possible level.

2.16   The Policy Meeting operated at two levels: a formal, minuted monthly meeting of the Policy Group, and a weekly, unminuted gathering which included the Governors 5 and focused on operational issues.

2.17   A recently-introduced, quarterly Central Management Team Meeting was to include all those managers who reported directly to a member of the Policy Group and additionally, Group Managers and the Security Principal Officer. This meeting provided a broad sounding board for managers and should improve lateral communications within the establishment.

2.18   The timetable for the other management meetings had been carefully planned to avoid clashes or overloading in particular weeks. A cycle had been developed with monthly meetings of the Policy Group, the Finance, Security and the Category A Review Committees, together with the Board of Visitors and the LRC. Bi-monthly meetings included the Race Relations Management Group, the Training Committee and the Chiltern Governors' Meeting. Quarterly meetings included Fire Prevention, the Local Whitley Council, the Health and Safety Committee and Occupational Health.

2.19   The day-to-day management of the establishment's budget had been delegated to the Finance Committee which was chaired by the HOMS. This involved all the members of the Policy Committee except the Governor. The Committee attempted to manage individual allocations by functional heads and to oversee the budget as a whole. Current thinking suggests that financial matters should be an item on the agenda of all functional and operational meetings because such an approach reinforces the importance of the financial dimension in decision making. We recommend that the work of the Finance Committee should be reviewed.

2.20   We noted that the Chairmen of the Race Relations Management Group and the Suicide Prevention Management Committee reported directly to the Governor - a clear indication of his commitment to these important areas of work.

2.21   Full staff meetings were held five or six times a year, and, when necessary, the staff were met before or after their shift or following an incident.

2.22   At the time of the inspection, there was no committee with inmate representatives, although the Governor recognised the value of such participation. The Race Relations Management Team had proposed the setting up of a Community Relations Group to be chaired by a Principal Officer with staff and inmate representatives. Standard items on the agenda would include the Shop, the library, diet, religious facilities, work and education. We thought this was a worthwhile proposal. We did not detect any reluctance on the part of the Governor for greater inmate participation. Inmates' opinions had been sought when there was a proposal to move the main meal of the day to tea time from lunch time. The Head of Custody regularly discussed institutional items with the Lifer Group. The Governor's primary concern was to invite and encourage more staff participation followed by increasing the degree of consultation with inmates.

2.23   There was a system of Governor's Orders and Notices to staff with General Notices to trainees. The Governor felt that these lacked definition and clarity and proposed to review them. We had noticed Governor's Orders in the Staff Information Room dating back to the early 1980s with no indication of those which were still current.

2.24   Meetings with staff representatives on the local Whitley Council were included in the meetings structure as was the formal, monthly meeting with the Prison Officers' Association.

Industrial relations
2.25   We met representatives of the following trade unions; the Prison Officers' Association (POA), the National Union of Civil and Public Servants (NUCPS) and the Union of Construction and Allied Trades Technicians (UCATT).

2.26   The POA spoke of the good relations they had with the Governor and of a number of local issues which were under discussion. They recognised the national staffing position but were convinced that Aylesbury was under staffed. The NUCPS representative referred to members dismay at the increasing differentials between their remuneration and that of the unified grades. There was a complaint that insufficient work was available in workshops, this could reduce further as a result of the proposed redevelopment. They also complained about the time taken by Headquarters to respond to staff matters; it was reported that a member of staff had been waiting 12 months for the outcome of a discipline enquiry. The local POA branch was uneasy about the monitoring of ethnic minorities which they felt could contribute to racial unrest. The UCATT representative made two points: one concerned the level of pay of UCATT members compared with trades officers and the other the lack of a promotion structure.

Section C   Staffing

Staff facilities

2.27   Staff facilities were generally good. Administrative staff had reasonable office accommodation, a rest room and a kitchen with microwave and refrigerator. In the wings, there were hot-water points and unisex toilets for staff use. Showers were in short supply, only F and G Wings shared such a facility. PE staff had to use the inmates' showers. We were told that staff showers were planned for the Emergency Control Room and visits; all this seemed rather vague and we therefore recommend that more showers are provided.

2.28   There was a Staff Mess and Staff Club just outside the Gate in separate but adjoining houses. Both were comfortably appointed; the former served mid-day and evening meals five days a week, while the latter was open from 11.30 am to 2.30 pm and from 7 pm to 11 pm every day. Both were used by single staff and by married staff living away from home. The Mess was well managed but the Club was, at the time of the inspection, the subject of a police investigation following an alleged misappropriation of funds. Staff were also able to use the establishment's sporting facilities when not being used by the inmates themselves. There was ample car-parking space.

Staff perceptions

2.29   We met a group of unified staff who made a number of points about the recent history of the institution, the impact of Fresh start, security and the need to retain positive control.

2.30   In their view, Aylesbury was a far better establishment than its reputation suggested and the institution's prevailing mood had improved over the last three or four years. Before that there had been a feeling that inmates, not staff, were in control. The improvement was attributed in part to a young and keen staff who, although they lacked experience, were enthusiastic and professional in their approach. Some staff missed the leadership of a Chief Officer; others, who had never experienced working under a Chief Officer, accepted the present situation without question. Fresh Start had brought many positive benefits in terms of time off but staffing problems existed. Top management were not considered to be aware of just how difficult things were and staff were managing to run the establishment on goodwill and flexibility alone.

2.31   There were concerns about perimeter security and the lack of searching of inmates after visits. Staff anxieties had been increased by the recent decision over the general cessation of censoring mail.

2.32   Staff were suspicious about the value of regime monitoring in that the measurements did not reflect what was actually happening. Finally, concern was expressed for the plight of the young staff posted to Aylesbury from the north and the difficulties they faced in attempting to find accommodation for themselves and their families. We shared this concern and believe further consideration should be given to the problem.

Staff complement and deployment
2.33   There was a complement of seven Governor grades, 11 Principal Officers, 20 Senior Officers and 140 Officers (including specialist grades). Total staff-in-post was therefore 98% of the establishment's target staffing figure in numerical terms. There was, however, a 28% deficiency at Senior Officer level which was covered by temporary or acting promotion from within the Officer complement (which had a surplus). The Officers were inexperienced with over half in their first two years of service. Providing cover for the shortfall of Senior Officers diminished still further, the already limited experience at Officer level. We felt that the vacancies at Senior Officer level should be filled through posting in of substantive ranks.

2.34   The discipline staff were divided into five Residential Groups and a single Operations Group, each under the management of a Principal Officer. The Inmate Activities and Services functions did not have their own group of discipline staff and were covered through cross deployment from the other groups. We regarded this outcome as unavoidable since a relatively small complement of staff can only be divided into a few groups if a realistic degree of self-sufficiency and accountability is to be maintained.

2.35   There was no properly structured programme for regular staff movement from group to group because of the differences in experience. This problem was being addressed and appropriate information had now been collated to allow individual career planning within the establishment. The establishment had a fairly high level of sick leave. This was not considered indicative of any complacency on the part of management in attempting to counter the problem.

Staff training

2.36   The Training Unit was on the second floor of the main institution block beside the Gate. It comprised a single classroom which was well equipped, bright and clean. This room doubled as an office and effective use was made of the available space. A small adjoining room had been adapted as a waiting area and doubled as a refreshment room.

2.37   Staff Training came under the Head of Management Services. The day-to-day running of the unit was the responsibility of a full-time Principal Officer. In addition to planning, co-ordinating and running training courses, the Training Principal Officer tested potential candidates wishing to join the Prison Service. This task was in addition to a substantial amount of induction work following the arrival of 42 new Officers in the year ending March 1991.

2.38   The availability of staff for local training posed problems but a lot of initiative had been used in producing training modules. These were not dependent on the number of participants and could be run at short notice. The range of training courses attended by staff was varied and the training hours achieved indicated support from management throughout the establishment. We were impressed with the recent introduction of a computer which will be used to store data and help identify the training needs of each individual member of staff.

CHAPTER THREE

INMATES

Section A   The inmate population

Inmate profile and catchment area

3.01   Aylesbury was a national resource for young offenders, including those in Category A, serving a wide range of sentence lengths from over three years up to, and including, life. The institution was not able to accept inmates requiring full-time medical supervision or nursing. Aylesbury was regarded as the most secure of the closed young offender establishments hence its acceptance of Category A inmates (we comment on security in paragraph 1.17 and in the Preface).

3.02   The recent conversion of The Mount Young Offender Institution (YOI) to an adult prison had resulted in the transfer of about 50 inmates to Aylesbury (some of whom had been serving sentences of under three years). The distribution of the population on 9 July 1991 is shown in Appendix 1. Including lifers, nearly three-quarters of the young men in the institution were serving sentences of more than four years. The age distribution showed nearly half (47%) were between 17 and 20 and 50% 20 or over.

3.03   We had some difficulty in understanding how the young offender system as a whole operated. No other YOI had exactly similar acceptance criteria and it seemed virtually impossible to transfer someone from Aylesbury to another YOI; instead they had to become adults on reaching 21 or be reclassified as such at an earlier date.

3.04   We question the wisdom and the propriety of one young offender establishment being regarded as the "end of the line" and the only one capable of holding Category A inmates. The difficulties faced by many visitors in reaching the institution were daunting, as was the prospect of individual inmates remaining in Aylesbury until a progressive move could be arranged. These factors together are considered sufficient to warrant a reappraisal of the system. In our experience, young offenders find it difficult to cope with long terms in custody. Three or four years to a 17 year old may seem a lifetime. The role of Aylesbury within the young offender estate needs to be more clearly defined. There is also a need to review allocation criteria, so that there is at least one other YOI to which inmates currently in Aylesbury (including Category As) could appropriately be sent.

Inmate perceptions
3.05   During the inspection, we met a group of inmates selected to represent their wings. They were, on the whole articulate and intelligent and were able to voice their opinions on a variety of issues, including the Woolf Report. In discussion, they made the following points:-

    a.   They should have a formal exercise period and were entitled to one hour's exercise daily in the open air.

    b.   Security had become too tight; staff would not move parties of inmates without permission from Control (ECR) and were over cautious and restrictive.

c.   The Education Department won unanimous
      approval along with the Braille Shop. Low
      pay for those on full-time education was,
      however, a disincentive.

d.   There was some criticism of staff for
      failing to recognise that not all inmates
      behaved like children; there was a tendency
      for inmates to be negatively stereotyped by
      staff.

e.   The lifers wanted a lifers-only wing and
      special privileges. They complained that
      they still had to wait too long to know the
      date of their first formal review.

f.   The group was suspicious of the grievance
      procedure. They saw it as more red tape
      and an opportunity to avoid responsibility.
      They were concerned that inmates pursuing
      complaints vigorously were in danger of
      becoming social outcasts.

g.   The Category A inmate complained about the
      time taken to obtain security clearance for
      his visitors and the general lack of
      privacy for Category A prisoners who were
      subjected to regular searches.

h.   Visiting conditions should be improved and
      there should be more time available for
      visitors.

i.   The Personal Officer scheme was welcomed,
      but there should be more psychiatric and
      psychological assistance available.

j.   There were complaints about the use of
      Control and Restraint procedures following
      the removal of a trainee to the Segregation
      Unit and after a recent hostage incident.

k.   The three trainees we met from ethnic
      minorities considered they were fairly
      treated and had no complaints.

Race Relations

3.06   The Race Relations Liaison Officer (RRLO) was a
Principal Officer who had been in post since November
1990; he had attended a race relations course at the
Prison Service College in Wakefield.

3.07   The Race Relations Management Team (RRMT) was
chaired by a Governor 5 from the residential staff group
and included the RRLO and his deputy, the Chaplain, the
Senior Probation Officer, the Senior Psychologist, the
Deputy Education Officer, the visiting Moslem minister
and a representative from Management Services. The RRMT
had also appointed one officer from each wing to act as
a representative and as the first point of contact for
inmates. Aylesbury's Statement of Purpose made specific
reference to race relations policy in stating that
varied opportunities would be offered to all inmates
regardless of ethnic origin.

3.08   The Psychology Department provided a quarterly
profile of the ethnic mix of inmates in the wings and
the workshop, and of those taking part in education and
physical education; it also looked at the ethnic
representation in disciplinary reports. It was planned
to produce more frequent profiles. The RRMT monitored
the reading material available in the library and took
an interest in issues related to the choice of food and
the provisions for worship. At the time of the

inspection, 32% of the total population were from ethnic minorities. The distribution within the accommodation was evenly balanced as was that amongst education and employment, except for the Painting and Decorating Course (see paragraph 3.10). Monitoring had also revealed an over-representation of ethnic minorities on minor reports in A, B and C Wings.

3.09   Inmates mixed freely in the wings with no evidence of racial conflict. A formal complaint by one inmate had been fully investigated and was found to be unjustified.

3.10   The Board of Visitors was concerned by a continuing under-representation of ethnic minorities on the Painting and Decorating Course which monitoring had confirmed. Even worse, the course ran below its capacity which was a waste of a valuable training resource. We recommend that the Governor looks into the reasons for this under-representation and also for the over-representation on minor reports.

3.11   We considered that all aspects of race relations and equal opportunities were well managed at Aylesbury. The staff were committed and the Race Relations Policy Statement was displayed at the Gate Lodge, in the Visiting Room, in the wings and elsewhere. Improvement objectives for Race Relations in the Governor's contract with his Area Manager included improving religious facilities and the system of Wing representatives and extending routine monitoring.

Section B   Settling-in

Reception
3.12   The Reception Unit was in a semi-basement near C Wing in what had been the Segregation Unit. All the

accommodation was in cells on one side of a narrow
corridor, the other side of which formed an outside
wall. The holding cells were bare and unwelcoming and
in need of redecoration, as was the entire Unit. Lack
of sufficient cells and storage space created problems.
For example, incoming inmates had to wait in a small
cell if there was any delay in processing outgoing
inmates.

3.13   The Unit was helped by the small numbers passing
through it and by the cheerful attitude of its staff who
did much to offset its rather grim appearance. Inmates'
property was properly stored but space was at a premium.
A local voucher system had been introduced to limit the
goods which the establishment could store.

3.14   We were not able to see the Unit in operation
but were confident that the staff treated the inmates
humanely. The new Reception Unit, to be included in the
Gate Complex (see paragraph 1.16) was probably several
years away; in the meantime, the reception area should
be thoroughly redecorated and refurbished. First
impressions are important and the Unit we saw, made it
much harder for staff to persuade inmates that Aylesbury
was a reasonable place in which to serve a sentence.

Induction and information to inmates
3.15   The Induction Unit was in a small spur on the
top floor of G Wing and consisted of an office and four
cells. The Unit's corridor was used for group sessions
because there was no class room. Two of the cells could
each take two inmates so that a maximum of six could be
accommodated at any one time. Any additional inmates
had to be located elsewhere - normally in A, B or C
Wings - and walk across to join induction sessions. The
Unit was rather bare and spartan in appearance; it
should be redecorated. It was also too small. We

recommend that it should be rehoused in larger premises as soon as a suitable opportunity arises during redevelopment.

3.16   What the Unit lacked in accommodation, it made up in its staff and programme. It was run by two keen young Officers and had a one-week programme during which those being inducted (as a group) met representatives of the specialist departments including Education, Physical Education, Psychology, Probation and the Chaplaincy. Staff saw their task as essentially threefold: to impart information to newly-arrived young men; to obtain information from them to check whether they were suited to the establishment (A, B and C); and to allay the often-encountered fears inmates had of the institution. We concluded that the staff were largely successful in completing these tasks; they certainly thought so and quoted sharply-reduced figures for young men requesting segregation for their own protection as one example of what they were achieving.

3.17   Much of what the inmates were told was backed up by written information available as handouts. These included a booklet produced by the Prison Service entitled 'Information for Young Offenders' and a locally-produced, twenty-four page, induction information booklet.

Sentence calculation
3.18   Sentences had been calculated in the sending establishments but were checked by an Administrative Officer in the Discipline Office. The second check was made by an Executive Officer and a final check by a Governor grade. Time spent in police custody was taken into account and inmates were informed of their release dates. Any subsequent changes - for example due to loss

of remission - were notified promptly. We were satisfied with the standard of documentation involved.

Allocation to accommodation

3.19   The system of allocating inmates to accommodation, following induction, was based on a simple assessment system which appeared to work very effectively. Aylesbury had formerly been two establishments and, despite the absence now of any physical barriers, remained so as far as accommodation was concerned. F and G Wings were some 250 yards from A, B and C Wings. During induction staff made an assessment of an inmate's likely ability to remain in normal location (A, B or C Wings). This was influenced by the nature of their offence, personality weaknesses and disorders, level of maturity and institutional experience. Those considered vulnerable were placed in F or G Wings, with lifers and inmates who were unlikely to pose any threat to the weaker element.

3.20   The above system of allocation greatly reduced the need to segregate inmates under Prison Rule 46 for their own protection. The division of inmates following induction seemed to be fairly common knowledge amongst the population but caused only minor problems occasionally in shared areas such as employment and education.

Inmate accommodation

3.21   Accommodation was, as stated above, in two separate buildings which had previously been independent penal institutions. What had once been a traditional local prison was now A, B and C Wings (near the main Gate) and the former female inebriate centre constituted F and G Wings.

3.22   Both accommodation buildings were substantially unaltered and were unsuitable for their present function. Single-cell accommodation was available for every inmate but there was no integral sanitation. The programme to instal integral sanitation throughout the institution was due to begin in G Wing in the near future. We inspected several cells and were impressed with their cleanliness and by the individuality introduced by some inmates.

3.23   F and G Wings each had 45 cells spread over three landings. Recesses provided toilet and slopping out facilities but were dirty and only superficially cleaned. Both F and G Wings were somewhat run down in appearance and urgently required the planned major refurbishment.

3.24   A and C Wings each had 67 cells while B Wing had 62; all were spread over three landings with the radial wings joining at a small Centre. The Centre had been gated off and the gates covered to prevent contact between inmates from different wings during association. Although a little better than F and G Wings, the recesses were not clean and close examination of most of the less obvious parts of A, B and C Wings revealed the dirt. The standard of cleanliness in communal and residential areas should be significantly improved.

Inmate facilities
3.25   Facilities were generally poor in all wings. Part of the problem was directly attributable to the design of the two old prisons which had been combined, many years ago, to function as a single establishment. While adult long termers in the dispersal system generally enjoy the best facilities available, their young counterparts in Aylesbury endure poorer conditions.

3.26   Space for association was particularly limited
on A, B and C Wings and was inadequate on F and G Wings.
Inmates on A, B and C Wings had the use of the floor
space of the ground floor landings of their respective
wings for association but there were no purpose built or
adapted rooms for use. Television, table tennis and
pool tables, had therefore to be placed on wing
thoroughfares as in some of the oldest local prisons.
F and G Wings shared a separate association room and
television room but these hardly met the needs of two
wings.

3.27   A system of split association was in operation
most of the week with the periods divided so that half
the inmates were out of their cells and the other half
locked-up. There was a changeover at set times during
each period. We felt that this had comparatively little
to do with the limited space available but was rather
more about staff availability. It was clear that new
association space was required urgently so that every
inmate could partake in full association.

3.28   We noted the absence of hot water boilers for
making drinks; they should be provided on each of the
wings. We should also like to see the hot cupboards in
the wing serveries used properly. The servery and wash-
up areas in F and G Wings should be kept clean.

Section C   Discipline and control

Good Order
3.29   Taken in isolation, the number of Governor's
Reports might lead an observer to conclude that the
establishment was controlled by disciplinary procedures.
The assumption is only partly correct.

3.30   Many of the population of Aylesbury were
immature. Most had committed serious offences involving
violence. The majority (72%) were serving sentences in
excess of four years. They were difficult, impulsive
and unpredictable.

3.31   The institution's recent history has been a
reflection of its difficult 'dispersal-type' population
and a period when staff felt they had not always been
fully in control. They believed they had since regained
control and there was a natural and understandable
reluctance to jeopardise that control.

3.32   In contrast to the above picture, we noted that
work was being undertaken by staff with individual
inmates. We observed healthy and positive contact
between staff and inmates on the wings, in the work
situation and in the classrooms. Staff seemed to have
achieved the fine balance of remaining firmly in control
whilst continuing to be sufficiently relaxed to allow a
discretionary element in their dealings with individual
inmates.

3.33   There remained an awareness from previous
experience (including the recent escape attempt
involving a hostage) that the potential for disruptive
and threatening behaviour remained.

Segregation Unit
3.34   The Segregation Unit was in the complex of
buildings clustered around A, B and C Wings; access was
via A Wing. The accommodation was in standard cells
without integral sanitation on two landings. Two cells
had been strengthened to Category A standard and two
others were unfurnished.

3.35   During the day, the Unit was supervised by a
Senior Officer and two Officers; at weekends this was
reduced. On weekday evenings the Unit was not
continuously staffed; between 4.30 and 7.30 pm it was
visited by staff from A Wing.

3.36   On the day the Unit was inspected, five trainees
were being held: two were segregated under Prison Rule
46 for good order and discipline; two were undergoing a
period of removal from the wings and the fifth was
awaiting adjudication. We were told this was an average
roll which documentation supported.

3.37   The Unit's regime was limited but flexible. The
adjoining exercise yard was temporarily out of use
because of building work involving scaffolding. Inmates
therefore exercised in an area next to C Wing. There
was no work other than cleaning but arrangements were
made to support inmates who were undertaking courses or
full-time education.

3.38   The documents to cover the use of non-medical
restraints had been recently introduced; no use of the
unfurnished cells had been recorded. Documents relating
to the use of Control and Restraint techniques were held
by the Governor 5, Head of Operations. The staff
Observation Book was fully maintained as was a Diary of
the routines and visitors to the Unit. Other
procedures, including the use of Rule 46, were examined
and found to be in order. In spite of the obvious
limitations, the atmosphere was good. The time and
trouble taken by staff was commendable. Our main
concerns were the periods during the evening and at
weekends when the Unit was only visited by staff, rather
than being patrolled. Given the inadequacy of the
hospital facility, disturbed inmates were occasionally
located in the Unit's unfurnished cells. Normally this

occurred at night when they could be supervised by a night patrol. However, the need for such a location might also occur during the evening period when supervision would be restricted to occasional visiting. Staffing levels in the Unit should be reviewed.

Adjudications

3.39   The figures for 1990/91 show a reduction in the number of adjudications (both Governor's and Board of Visitors') compared to those of the previous year.

Year	Average population	Number of Governors Adjudications	Number of Board of Visitors Adjudications	Number of Adjudications per inmate
1989/90	266	1,282	19	4.8
1990/91	241	1,160	9	4.8

Note. In each year one offence was prosecuted at court.

However because the average number of inmates had also been lower, the rate of offending had remained unchanged at the high level of 4.8 reports per trainee. This is considered indicative of the difficulties generated by a young population.

3.40   The Psychological Services Department had examined a number of factors relating to Governor's and minor reports between 1986 and 1991. An examination of their data revealed:-

> a.   a tendency to use Governor's reports rather than minor reports against a general decline in the overall rate of reporting;

> b.   an increased number of Governor's reports;

> c.   a marked decrease in minor reports;

d. a reduction in Governor's reports involving violence; and

e. a reduction in the number of assaults on staff.

3.41 A number of adjudication records (Forms 256) were examined; the hearing of adjudications was evenly divided between the Governor, the Head of Custody and the Head of Inmate Activities. The standard of documentation was generally satisfactory but we noted a few minor errors and some variation in the length of the record of the hearings. We also noted a wide variation in the punishment awards and considered some on the high side for the offences committed. We therefore recommend that the Governor should review local procedures for reporting offences, arrange for regular scrutiny of adjudication records and meet periodically with adjudicating officers to review levels of award and ensure consistency of practice.

3.42 We sat in on a number of hearings and found them to be satisfactory and in keeping with the general tone of the establishment.

Escape List
3.43 At the time of the inspection, no inmates were subject to Escape List restrictions. The Escape List had been used and we were advised that when this happened, the same procedures as for adults was followed.

Closed Visits
3.44 There were no facilities for closed visits - ie where a complete physical barrier separates the inmate from his visitors. What were classed as closed visits took place in a bare room off the main corridor leading

to the Centre (ie the conjunction of A, B and C Wings). Security was provided by close staff supervision rather than by any physical barrier. Proper closed visiting facilities should be provided and there should be a designated private area in which inmates could be searched before and after visits.

Searching

3.45   The searching programme was built around a local division of the population into three groups: Category A inmates, other high risk inmates (ie those serving sentences of over 7 years), and lower risk (ie everyone else). The cells of Category A inmates were searched every two weeks; the individuals concerned changed cells monthly. The cells of other high risk trainees were searched once a month and those of lower risk, about every three months on a random basis.

3.46   Inmates were given a rub-down search after visits and more thoroughly searched if there was a suspicion that trafficking had taken place. A metal detection portal was used for visitors entering the establishment and we were told that property received was searched with the aid of a hand-held metal detector.

Drugs

3.47   Drugs did not appear to be a significant problem. There had been only 12 recorded drug finds in 1990/91. The general feeling was that inmates did not have the resources for sustained drug taking. A recent search of the establishment by a drug team had not found any drugs or any indication of drugs. This had supported the local assumption of the comparative rarity of drugs in the institution.

CHAPTER FOUR

REGIME

Section A   Routines

Association

4.01   There was no association on Saturday and Sunday evenings and little more than an hour on other evenings of the week. We calculated that inmates could spend little more than 32 hours out of their cells in an average week. This was a very disappointing level of activity for young men most of whom were serving long sentences (see also paragraphs 3.26 and 3.27).

4.02   Staffing levels for evening association appeared too high under the 'split system' used. On one occasion we noted four officers supervising thirteen inmates. We discussed this with staff, suggesting that manning levels for association were probably higher than in adult establishments caring for the same type of inmate. There was a view that the high manning level was necessary because Aylesbury housed some of the most dangerous, volatile and unpredictable inmates in the prison system. There were some very difficult young men in the institution but we felt that they could be more easily persuaded to behave well if the regime was not so impoverished. We therefore recommend that all inmates should receive the full period of association every evening of the week.

Exercise

4.03   There was not a scheduled programme to provide inmates with exercise, in the open air on a daily basis. On most days, 'exercise' comprised of the time taken to walk to and from places of employment and other activities. It is important that inmates are offered the opportunity of one hour's exercise (weather permitting) in the fresh air every day.

Meal times

4.04   Meal times were as set out in the table below:-

Meal	Weekday	Weekend
Breakfast	8.25	8.15
Dinner	11.45	11.15
Tea	4.00	3.35

As in so many other establishments, we found the timing of the second and third meals of the day far too early and the corresponding intervals between meals - 17 hours from Sunday tea to Monday breakfast - too long. It was clear that meals were timed to suit staff shifts rather than inmates' needs. We recommend that the mid-day and evening meals be served substantially later in the day. We were told that plans to make the third meal the main meal of the day had not met with much enthusiasm from inmates and had therefore been postponed. We hope that the proposed Community Relations Group - which might begin meeting bi-monthly from as early as September 1991 with inmate representatives - will consider this again; this change has proved popular with inmates in other establishments. But even if tea becomes the main meal, meal times remain unfair and unhealthy.

Section B   Services

Pay and private cash

4.05   Pay rates were those prescribed by the Prison Service and were uniformly low, ranging from about £1.75 to £5.75 per week. Inmates were allowed to spend up to £10 per month private cash (to a maximum of £120 per year); they were advised when they had spent between £92 and £100 in order to encourage budgeting before the annual limit was reached. There were relatively few problems with private cash from sending establishments and Aylesbury took care to ensure the private cash of its inmates was forwarded within a week of transfer.

Shop

4.06   The Shop was at the end of a series of adjoining buildings connected to F and G Wings. The accommodation was spacious but poorly decorated and unimaginatively laid out. No price and stock list existed, although prices were displayed on the shelving. The Shop was open to inmates from A, B and C Wings on Monday, Tuesday and Wednesday mornings, and on Saturday mornings to inmates from F and G Wings. Each inmate was able to visit the Shop once a week and could spend both prison earnings and private cash. In the hospital and the Segregation Unit, inmates ordered goods which were delivered.

4.07   The range of goods stocked was on the low side, numbering little more than 120 lines - this could, however, be supplemented to some extent by special orders eg vegan chocolate. Fresh fruit was neither stocked, nor available on special order. Staff were aware of the Shop's deficiencies and had begun to make changes to bring about improvements. They had realised that the local 'cash and carry' store from which they had ordered goods was not providing a good service and were therefore increasingly turning to other outlets. We welcomed advanced, local plans to purchase a fridge-freezer so that goods like ice cream, yoghurts, fresh milk and fresh fruit could be stocked. Health and safety guidelines will need to be strictly followed.

4.08   More, however, needed to be done. We recommend that the Shop be thoroughly redecorated and better laid out. It should carry a larger range of stock, including more ethnic and vegan items. Two Officers ran the Shop full-time with a third used as a 'runner' to escort inmates. Whilst an Officer presence in the Shop is desirable, we thought there was scope for partial civilianisation. We also wondered whether it was advisable for the Shop staff to work out inmates' pay from the party sheets; consideration should be given to this work being done by administrative staff.

Clothing and Kit

4.09   Inmates were not allowed to wear their own clothing. They were given institutional clothing on arrival - a typical issue included, inter alia, three pairs of socks and underpants, four shirts and two towels. The institution aimed to change two of each item each week during kit exchange which took place in the wings at weekends. We were told that these exchanges were not as carefully supervised by staff as they should be, as a result, exchanges were not made on a one-for-one basis. Kit "losses" were high, although it was likely that most of the "missing" items were in inmates' cells. A recent kit search of the wings had revealed some items over and above the official allowance but not to the extent that might have been expected. It may be that more frequent thorough kit searches needed to be mounted. Staff should exercise better control over the arrangements for kit exchange.

4.10   No personal kit system operated despite Aylesbury being a long-term training establishment and having its own laundry. We see advantages in the introduction of such a system and recommend accordingly. The establishment did not seem to benefit from its laundry. The latter served a number of other establishments and, we were told, regarded Aylesbury as no more than one contract among a number. We accept

that laundries must fulfil contractual obligations, and
have taken into account the laundry's particular
difficulties, but where an establishment has its own
laundry, some degree of priority may perhaps be given to
its own washing.

Catering

4.11   A Senior Officer, four Officers and fourteen
inmates worked in the kitchen; two of the latter were
employed solely as cleaners and three were from ethnic
minorities. All the catering staff had completed health
and hygiene training, as had nine of the inmates. The
Education Department organised such training for inmates
on the Catering Vocational Training Course (VTC) and
those involved in serving food in the wings. The
training of kitchen inmates needed to be reviewed to
ensure continuity. Consideration should be given to the
introduction of the Caterbase NVQ course, despite the
existence of the Catering VTC.

4.12   Kitchen inmates worked a seven day week from
about 7 am to 12 noon and again from 1 to 4.30 pm with
breaks mid-morning and mid-afternoon. They could have
two hourly sessions of PE each week and one half day
each weekend. The inmate changing area was in very poor
condition, with missing floor tiles, peeling paintwork
and bare timber. It should be refurbished. We were
pleased to see that kitchen inmates had their own
showers. Meals were transported from the kitchen to the
wings by heated trolleys and, in the case of A, B and C
Wings, by means of a lift. We sampled the second meal
of the day on the Tuesday of our inspection when the
following was on offer: beef curry and rice, steamed
bacon roll, creamed potatoes, turnip, cabbage, a soya
dish (the vegetarian alternative) and jam scones. The
potatoes were so lumpy as to be inedible - a new supply
had to be prepared at the last moment, delaying the

timing of the meal. The potatoes were from Hollesley Bay, many of them were bad and inedible on arrival. The fault was said to be due to the poor quality product and poor cooking by inmates. We were not impressed by the sweet, the scone was dry and hard. We concluded that efforts needed to be made to improve the quality of the meals. It would assist if the dietary scales for young offenders were increased.

4.13   The kitchen was of a reasonable size and well equipped and laid out. It was fairly clean only in the most accessible areas. The general standard of cleanliness needed to be improved. There was evidence of cockroaches; this infestation should be eradicated. Cross-contamination of different foodstuffs was a potential hazard in the vegetable area. The fridge did not appear to be operating at a sufficiently low temperature. We noted both cooked foods, uncooked foods and dairy products were stored together; alternative arrangements should be made.

Legal aid and appeals
4.14   A legal aid service was provided by the Residential Senior Officers, eight of whom were trained. There was no designated Legal Aid Officer, nor a Legal Aid Office. However, the number of legal aid applications was so small that the existing arrangements appeared satisfactory. Most of the young men arriving at Aylesbury had already appealed against their conviction or sentence and relatively few were married or had domestic legal matters to resolve. We were told that on average, only two legal aid applications were made each month.

Privileges
4.15   The institution had an official list of those items which inmates were allowed to have in their

possession, together with an indication of how they might be obtained. The list was widely publicised throughout the establishment. We considered the range of items reasonable for a long-term establishment. The limited association facilities are dealt with at the start of this chapter and in paragraphs 3.26 and 3.27.

Requests and complaints procedures

4.16   Since 1 January 1991, 85 Request and Complaints forms had been issued, of which 61 had been returned completed. The requests and complaints process was co-ordinated by the Head of Custody and the register maintained by staff in the Discipline Office. Examination of this showed that inmates had taken advantage of their right of confidential written access to the Governor and the Area Manager. One inmate had requested a confidential interview with the Chairman of the Board of Visitors. Most complaints related to transfers, treatment, and property queries. Issues which could be dealt with locally - the majority - were being resolved within seven days. Replies from Headquarters took longer and interim responses were issued.

4.17   When we took views from inmates (see paragraph 3.05), they said they were not convinced of the value of the request/complaints procedures. We have found this is not uncommon among young offenders who tend to be reluctant to commit themselves to writing and are suspicious of those that do. Our experience suggests that inmates would much rather talk to staff about their difficulties than fill in forms.

Section C   Activities

Employment

4.18   An Occupation Profile is at Appendix 3.
Employment of an industrial nature was limited to one
Prison Service Industries and Farms (PSIF) workshop and
a laundry. The PSIF workshop is shown on the profile as
EME (ie its previous function - Electro-Mechanical
Engineering) although it had for some time been a
Contract Services shop. Unfortunately, there had been
an acute shortage of work in the shop for some months
despite efforts by PSIF's sales representatives. The
workshop would normally expect to employ 36 inmates
(Effective Minimum Complement). We saw the three
instructors (all qualified engineers who had been
retained when the shop switched to contract services)
and two inmates with absolutely nothing to do. In
desperation, one of the inmates had volunteered to clean
the copper pipes under the shop's wash-hand basins. The
instructors were demoralised. We appreciate the
difficulty in finding suitable outside contracts. These
difficulties may be exacerbated during a recession.
However, unless a steady supply of good quality work can
be maintained we doubt the value of retaining any PSIF
shop. In such circumstances, it might be better to
replace the shop with additional Vocational Training
(VT) and Construction Industry Training (CIT) courses.
A charity-type workshop, involved with the local
community, may also be able to provide work for inmates.

4.19   The laundry employed two instructors and about
14 inmates. It washed Aylesbury's laundry and that of a
number of other establishments, including The Mount.
Some of the equipment was obsolete but was scheduled to
be replaced. We noted that inmate labour was not
available to the laundry for half a day during the

inspection. Every effort should be made to maintain inmate staffing levels to ensure the laundry operates as productively as possible.

4.20   We were concerned with the way the laundry washed soiled and foul linen. Guidance on this subject is available to NHS laundries in Health Circular (87)30. This would not be suitable for Prison Service laundries but we believe PSIF could usefully issue clear mandatory instructions, distilled from this Circular, to all Laundry managers.

Farms and gardens
4.21   The institution had no farming enterprise. A considerable number of lawns and flowerbeds were showing signs of neglect. An inmate might easily hide amongst the weeds and shrubbery. The institution had been without a garden's officer for a considerable period. An officer and a small party of inmates were working on the grounds when we inspected.

Education
4.22   The Education Department was housed in a modern, purpose-built, two-storey block with ten classrooms. Staff facilities were satisfactory. The only problem was ventilation in the summer due to small windows. The Department was run by five full-time teachers (including the Education Officer and her Deputy) and about 25 part-time staff. A major difficulty was the absence of any administrative support. The Education officer was herself having to do routine administrative work or ask teachers to do it with a consequent loss of contact time with students. Adequate administrative assistance should be provided (but see paragraph 2.08). There were good links with the nearby Aylesbury College of Further Education. An Education Consultative Committee met twice a year.

4.23   Participation in education was entirely
voluntary. The Department was by far the largest
employer in the institution. About 45 inmates were on
full-time education (ie they had to attend eight out of
ten weekly sessions) and a further 15 were part-timers.
In addition, up to 58 further inmates could be engaged
on Vocational Training Courses - see paragraph 4.26.
The daytime teaching year ran Monday to Friday for 46
weeks each year; the evening year was three days a week
for 36 weeks. We were told it was proposed to increase
the former by two weeks to 48 weeks. We should like to
see the latter increased to four evenings a week.
Inmates from F and G Wings could then attend evening
education on at least two evenings a week.

4.24   Among the courses available were General Basic
Studies including English, numeracy, social skills,
handicrafts and cookery and a Business and Finance
course. The former led to a certificate and the latter
to a diploma. Inmates successfully completing the
Business course could go on to take further, more
advanced courses on release. Other courses included
French, German, music, art, pottery, soft toy-making,
biology, creative writing and yoga. A small number of
inmates were studying for A levels in a total of 11
different subjects. For them, tutors came in especially
and full-time education staff also acted as wing tutors
and liaised closely with inmates' Personal Officers.
Open University studies were also available to the most
able; four inmates had been enrolled in the previous
year (three had now gone on to the adult system). Open
learning material was also available.

4.25   We concluded that inmates were being offered a
good range of appropriate courses and that the Education

Department would continue to play a crucial role in occupying a considerable proportion of the institution's population.

Vocational Training Courses

4.26   Five Vocational Training Courses (VTCs) were available: Braille, Catering, Engineering Drawing Office Skills (EDOS), Electronic Wiring and Electronic Servicing. The last four courses could employ up to ten inmates each, while the Braille course could take up to 18 young men. The falling population and natural wastage meant that the average total number of inmates engaged in these five courses was about 40 (or just under 70%). We should like to see a higher percentage take-up rate of what were expensive course places.

4.27   We considered the Braille, Catering and EDOS courses to be worthwhile. The first translated books into Braille were under contract to various bodies including the Royal National Institute for the Blind. The Braille Workshop needed better equipment such as window screening and proper desks, chairs and book rests for the computers it used. The Catering course supplied a number of trained workers to the kitchen. The EDOS course had recently introduced computerised engineering drawing and had won the 1990 Peter Guise Memorial Prize for the best VT course. We shared the Education Officer's doubts about the two, not entirely complementary, electronic courses. Consideration might be given to replacing at least one of these courses with, for example, computer, office or business skills training, or motor mechanics - all of which might have more appeal to young men. There was a need for one or two more courses which would allow inmates to use their hands to a greater extent.

Construction Industry Training (CIT) Courses

4.28   There was only one CIT Course, Painting and Decorating. Attendance was poor with only four inmates on a course which could cater for twelve. The pass rate for the Course's City and Guilds examination was low. Although the accommodation was good, the course participants appeared to lack enthusiasm. Despite the lack of other CIT Courses, Painting and Decorating was not a popular course at Aylesbury.

4.29   We should like to see at least one additional CIT course introduced - bricklaying may be the most beneficial to inmates and the establishment.

Library

4.30   There was no central library which inmates could visit. Instead, the principal library was in G Wing (for F and G Wings) with separate libraries in A, B and C Wings. The numbers and condition of books were reasonable. Access to the libraries was daily during the week. Conditions in each could be improved in terms of decoration and by providing easy chairs and tables. With no central library, work or other daily activities had to be interrupted and in the evenings or weekends (when inmates were more readily available) existing staff shift patterns often complicated matters.

4.31   The establishment had recognised the current position as being unsatisfactory. The creation of a central reference library restricted, essentially, to inmates in education - was only a partial answer as the Education officer acknowledged. We consider that one central library should be established. It should be properly equipped and furnished with adequate space for inmates to browse and take notes. The number of staff required to supervise this activity should be established and appropriate shift patterns examined.

Physical Education

4.32   Aylesbury had a small, purpose-built gymnasium
(dating from the early 1960s), a separate good-sized
weights room, a large grass sports field and a small
unheated open air swimming pool. The showers in the
gymnasium were in need of refurbishment. The seven PE
staff ran a full programme of sporting activities
including football, volley ball, basket ball,
weightlifting, rugby and cricket (during the summer). A
copy of the PE programme is at Appendix 6. Weekday
activities were mainly party-based, while those in the
evenings were club-or-activity-based. Inmates were
allowed two hours voluntary PE during the working week.
Evening PE, which was available five days a week, was by
application and waiting list. Community Sports Leaders
Award courses and GCSE O level classes were available.

4.33   Sporting provision at Aylesbury was reasonable.
The size of the gymnasium limited both the activities
which could be offered and the number of inmates who
could participate. Redevelopment should, in due course,
include the provision of a purpose-built sports hall.
Only very limited use could be made of the swimming
pool; it should be covered, heated and have changing and
showering facilities. A similar pool in Maidstone
prison had been improved at very modest cost and was now
used throughout the year.

Religious activities

4.34   The Church of England Chaplain held a full-time
post. The Roman Catholic and Methodist Chaplains were
both part-time and able to spend little time in the
institution. The Chaplain encouraged young theological
students to join him in the institution and they were a
valuable asset. The bishop was reported to be very
supportive and contact with the local church was good.

4.35   The number of inmates in minority faiths was
small, the largest being a dozen Muslims. An Imam
visited infrequently from London; the inmates met
together for prayers each week. Sikh and Buddhist
Ministers visited as necessary. There was no multi-
faith room although staff were said to be very co-
operative in allowing the use of interview and other
rooms. We consider a multi-faith room should be
provided in due course.

4.36   There was a Church of England service every
Sunday at 9.30 am and a Roman Catholic Mass at 10.45 am;
both were held in the institution's small Chapel.
Muslim inmates met every Friday and Sikhs each Monday -
the latter group meeting was sometimes attended by Hindu
inmates. Attendance at the two main Christian services
ranged from 35 to 50 and from 15 to 25 respectively.
Two discussion groups were run, one for the main prison,
the other for F and G Wings - both involved outside
speakers and operated waiting lists.

4.37   The Chaplain spent a lot of time in the wings
and usefully promoted work with the institution's lifers
and Category A inmates. We concluded that religious
activities were in a satisfactory state.

Community activities
4.38   The establishment's occupation profile made
provision for three inmates to be engaged full-time in
community activities outside the perimeter. At the time
of the inspection, one worked in a playgroup, one in an
old people's home and one with Community Service
Volunteers. The seriousness of the offences committed
by the population made any further development
difficult, as did the tight budget for inmates'
travelling and subsistence. Two groups of disabled
children and adults regularly visited the establishment.

Selected inmates worked with them on a one to one basis. This initiative had culminated in a Day of Experience which had been attended by nearly 400 such children and 50 inmates.

Regime monitoring

4.39   The Head of Inmate Activities (HIA) took a close interest in regime monitoring. Returns from the various areas of the prison went to an Administrative Assistant for inputting to the computer. The standardised, computer printouts were circulated to the Governor and functional heads and discussed at the weekly SMG. The HIA was satisfied that the information produced was reasonably accurate (given the well-known and widely acknowledged limitations of the present system). The institution's recent average of 21½ inmate hours of activity each week was better than the corresponding total of 15.2 hours for 1989/90. A considerably higher target was both necessary and attainable.

CHAPTER FIVE

RESETTLEMENT

Section A   Family Links

Visits

5.01   Many visitors came long distances but there were
no amenities outside the institution. The latest
indications are that a Visitors Centre was not included
in the plans for the Gate complex. We consider this
disappointing and recommend a review of the plans.
Visits were held in a large first-floor room above
offices near A, B and C Wings and opposite the Gate.
Visiting times were from 1.15 to 3.15 pm on Wednesday,
Saturday and Sunday afternoons. However, the process of
getting people in and out of the prison effectively
restricted these times to between 1.30 and 3 pm.
Inmates could have two visits every 28 days but there
was no guarantee that each visit would last for a
complete 90 minute period. The numbers of visitors at
weekends sometimes meant that individual visits were
limited to one hour. This is not acceptable. Weekend
visiting times should be extended by at least half an
hour (with routines and shift patterns adjusted
accordingly, if necessary). Although most visits will
continue to take place at weekends, some further
pressure would be taken off this period if visits were
allowed every day of the week - we recommend
accordingly.

5.02   Visiting conditions were poor. The visits room
was shabby in appearance and uncarpeted, with old and
uncomfortable hard chairs and tables. Refreshments were
available from a bar run by the Women's Royal Voluntary
Service. There was nowhere for young children to play.

The planned new Gate complex would provide purpose-built
visiting facilities. These were some time away and we
recommend that the existing facilities should be
redecorated and that comfortable, easy chairs and low
coffee tables be provided.

Letters and telephones
5.03   Routine censoring of inmates correspondence
(except for Category A inmates) had ended on 23 June
1991, in accordance with Prison Service guidelines.
There were no restrictions on the length of incoming or
outgoing letters or on the number of letters inmates
could receive or send (subject to paying postage
charges).

5.04   The institution did not have card phones when we
inspected. However plans had been made and an order
placed for their provision in 1992. If possible, we
should like to see greater priority given to this
project. Until that time, calls using official
telephones would continue to be made on behalf of
inmates by staff as necessary.

Prison Visitors
5.05   The number of Prison Visitors had increased
under the present Chaplain from five to 30, of whom
three were from ethnic minorities. There was still a
waiting list of inmates wanting a Prison Visitor, and
the Chaplain was aware of the need to recruit more
members - especially from ethnic minorities. Inmates
saw Prison Visitors in the visiting room without having
to surrender a visiting order.

Section B   Throughcare

Personal Officer Scheme and review procedures

5.06   The development of a more comprehensive personal officer scheme was a priority of the Governor. Local training had begun for staff to increase their awareness of the importance of the scheme and their confidence in handling the responsibilities it carried. Each inmate was allocated a personal officer who was responsible, with the appropriate Probation Officer, for his welfare needs. Personal Officers also had a responsibility to review their inmates informally twice a year and to attend formal review boards. The full review system involved the inmate being interviewed by a panel which included the wing Principal Officer, a Probation Officer and other specialists as required. These review boards provided an opportunity to update the inmate's sentence plan which had been outlined during the induction period.

Probation

5.07   The Probation Department came under the Head of Custody and comprised a Senior Probation Officer (SPO) and four Probation Officers, all of whom were from the Buckinghamshire County Probation Service. It was not clear whether the latter seconded staff compulsorily or not; we were, however, advised that the officers in post were all volunteers.

5.08   A contract between the Chief Probation Officer and the Governor for the work to be undertaken by seconded probation staff and the facilities to be provided by the Governor was almost complete. The Statement of Purpose and the Aims of the Probation Service, together with the principal activities related to both, had been documented in April 1991. This was closely followed by a document prepared by the SPO and the Head of Custody which described the contribution of the seconded probation team to the contract between the Governor and the Area Manager. This document took each function of the establishment, described the Probation Department's main contribution and set out baseline and key indicators. Together these papers were a clear statement of joint working and provided a framework for probation work at Aylesbury.

5.09   The SPO was involved in the general management of the establishment through his functional head and by his membership of the Regimes Committee, the Race Relations Management Team and attendance at other meetings. We considered that potential existed for increased involvement and we recommend that this be explored further.

5.10   All Probation Officers had at one time been wing-based; when we inspected, only some were wing-based, due to the inadequacy of the office accommodation in the wings. An office for probation staff should be available in each wing. Wing Probation Officers made an important contribution to the Sentence Planning Boards which were the formal contact point for probation staff and Personal Officers. Informal day-to-day contacts were frequent. Personal Officers increasingly discussed inmates' emotional or family problems, in confidence, with Probation Officers (including 'home' Probation Officers). These developments went a considerable way towards fulfilling the requirements of Circular Instruction (CI) 40/1988 which places responsibility for throughcare with the Prison Service. This progress should continue.

5.11   There were groups on offending behaviour, drugs, alcohol abuse, racial awareness and coping with custody; but none looking at adolescent sex offending. This was an area where training (for staff) was lacking and where the national initiative concentrated on adult offenders. It was clear that such training was necessary if staff were to have any chance of helping this type of Young Offender.

5.12   The SPO monitored weekly the tasks completed by his staff but needed the appropriate administrative support to continue doing so. We regard administrative support to the Probation Department as essential to allow probation staff to concentrate on their primary tasks.

Psychological Services Department

5.13   The Psychological Services Department was regarded as a separate function. The Principal Psychologist reported directly to the Governor and was a member of the Policy Group. The remaining staff of the Department comprised two Senior Psychologists, a Higher Psychologist, a Psychologist and a Psychological Assistant. In addition to the work undertaken at Aylesbury, a visiting service was provided for Littlehey and to other establishments on request. Like their probation colleagues, the psychologists required wing interview facilities.

5.14   The work of the department fell under three broad headings:-

    a.   **inmate counselling and clinical support**
          This included individual counselling and group work in such areas as temper control, personal development, stress, depression, and sexual problems. From this had come involvement and participation in the

sentence planning and review processes
together with working alongside and
supporting Personal Officers.

b.   **management consultancy**
The Department was represented on the
Policy Group, Regimes Meetings, the Race
Relations and the Suicide Prevention
Management Groups, the Training, Research
and Development and Occupational Health
Committees.

c.   **management information**
Quarterly surveys of the inmate population
were completed and the information
presented in graphical form. A survey of
staff training projects had been completed
and further surveys were planned.

5.15   As the pace of the Personal Officer scheme had
increased, psychologists had identified a need to
clarify the areas of work undertaken by the different
specialists. It may be that individual inmates are
being seen by a number of staff without the necessary
co-ordination taking place. Better co-ordination could
be combined with a more systematic approach to the
Sentence Planning Boards looking at matters like the
date of the last review, how often the inmate saw his
Personal Officer and the extent to which he understood
the targets set for him. This recommended approach
would be more objective and should allow for a better
appraisal of progress.

5.16   We concluded that the department had achieved a
proper balance between research, the collection and
presentation of management information and therapeutic

work with inmates. Participation in staff training and increasing involvement with Personal Officers and other specialists were particularly important.

Local Review Committee

5.17   We met the Chairman of the Local Review Committee (LRC). There were six LRC members from the Board of Visitors, eight from the Probation Service, and seven independent members. In the year ending 31 December 1990, all eligible cases (123) had been considered for parole; of these, 52 had been recommended, and 44 eventually granted parole.

5.18   The Chairman was generally content with the way the work was undertaken. The 50 or so inmates transferred from The Mount had resulted in additional work and some late reviews. It was not uncommon for those transferred from other establishments to arrive with incomplete parole documentation, thereby increasing the workload on Aylesbury. With regard to entries made in inmates' records, the Chairman felt that staff tended to report only negative occurrences and, in doing so, failed to provide a balanced view of performance.

Recategorisation and transfer

5.19   Most of the inmates in Aylesbury were serving long sentences for serious offences, many involving violence. It was not surprising that few progressed to open conditions. A decision was made several weeks before an inmate was formally reclassified as an adult prisoner about his allocation within the adult system. There were, however, difficulties in transferring certain reclassified inmates and particularly those in Category A. We consider that it is unhelpful both to the establishment and to the individuals concerned, to delay such transfers unless there are good reasons in the inmate's interest.

Temporary release

5.20   Most temporary releases were made in connection
with the community attachments described in paragraph
4.38. The nature of the population severely limited the
use which could be made of temporary release and, while
each case was considered on its merits, most inmates who
went outside the establishment's walls did so under
escort.

Pre-release

5.21   Very few inmates were discharged from Aylesbury
on completion of sentence; a large number passed into
the adult system. Efforts had been made, to incorporate
much of the material from the standard pre-release
course in an inmate's personal development course. A
lot of work had been done by the four Officers who had
attended the pre-release trainers course. The Senior
Probation Officer had provided a great deal of support.
It was hoped to increase the current one week course for
inmates to two weeks, with a greater emphasis on the
needs of those facing a long period in custody.

CHAPTER SIX

MEDICAL AND SPECIAL FEATURES

Section A   Medical Services

Staffing

6.01   The part-time Medical Officer (MO) was a General Practitioner (GP) from a local practice. The MO was contracted to attend for ten hours each week; in practice attendance was shared on an ad hoc basis by all the GPs in the practice - one disadvantage of this arrangement was that hospital staff seldom knew in advance which doctor would be on duty. The MO provided night and weekend on-call cover.

6.02   Two of the MO's contracted hours were for management work but he did not attend meetings of the Senior Management Group; we recommend that he is encouraged to do so. The General Practice was about to become a budget-holder under the NHS re-organisation and we therefore recommend that it should be invited to provide services in physiotherapy, chiropody and minor operations at the same time it would be necessary for appropriate funding to be made available.

6.03   Staffing in the hospital comprised a Hospital Senior Officer and three Hospital Officers, one of whom was a qualified nurse. They worked during the day but there was no night cover; at night the hospital was patrolled by the night patrol officer who also covered F and G Wings. He had a rest room with cooking facilities in the hospital itself.

The Hospital

6.04   Hospital accommodation was on two-floors above the Reception Unit in buildings between the Gate and C Wing (but adjoining the latter). On the ground floor, there was a pharmacy/treatment room and a dental surgery/optician's room together with an office for the hospital staff. On the first-floor, there were three cells containing a total of four beds and two offices (at least one office was never used). If possible, unused accommodation in the hospital should be reallocated for other purposes. Consideration should be given to refitting safety netting across the space opposite these cells. This would prevent the risk of death or injury resulting from someone jumping over the low railing to the ground floor.

6.05   The hospital was little used with only 12 admissions in the six months before the inspection. In 1990 however, there had been 120 visits to outside hospitals, the staff escort costs will have been considerable. We wondered whether all these outside referrals had been necessary with a view to increasing the use of in-patient facilities (despite their limitations). The need for so many patients to be referred should be examined.

6.06   The Medical Officer saw on average between four and six inmates at the weekday surgeries. We considered this to be a low number (even after taking into account that young offenders were comparatively fit) and wondered if inmates were, in any way, being discouraged from seeing the MO. This should not, of course, happen: all inmates should have unimpeded access to the Medical Officer.

6.07   We considered the hospital to be a poor facility. If Aylesbury is to continue as a national resource for long-term young offenders and subject to any change of role arising from reconsideration of it role (see paragraph 3.04) we believe it should have a properly equipped Medical Centre with a full-time Medical Officer and night cover.

Pharmacy

6.08   The treatment room was in the pharmacy. This is not acceptable - a separate treatment room should be established. Pharmaceutical supplies were obtained weekly from nearby Grendon Prison. Limited self-medication had been admirably developed. Stock control was computerised and inmates were normally allowed a seven-day supply of the particular medication they had been prescribed. This had details of the drug, the dosage and the inmate's name and number on a printed label. A simple but very effective colour coding system operated; yellow labels denoted inmates considered suitable for self-medication and therefore allowed to have the medication in possession whilst pink labels indicated those who were not. We recommend that Aylesbury's system of self medication should be offered for wider application.

Dental services

6.09   We were not readily able to determine how often or for how long the part-time Dental Officer (a visiting local dentist) attended; professional visits like these should be more identifiably recorded at the Gate. We eventually determined that the Dental Officer attended for two hours, twice-weekly and saw, on average about six patients each session. Despite this and the absence of any elaborate conservation work, there was a two-month waiting list for treatment. This was, in our view, too long. We suggest the Dental Officer sees more patients per session and that the waiting list is reduced. Long-termers and lifers should be called up automatically every six months for check-ups.

6.10   We saw only two dental handpieces in the surgery which we were told the dentist had supplied. Three complete sets of sterilisable handpieces should be provided by the prison. We were disturbed to discover an ethyl chloride spray in one of the dental trays and to be told it was used. Ethyl chloride was formerly used to induce general anaesthesia or localised absence of sensation by 'freezing'. It is ineffective as a local anaesthetic, inflammable and dangerous if sprayed into the mouth. The spray should be removed from the surgery and disposed of safely.

Psychiatric services
6.11   A retired consultant psychiatrist visited the institution weekly for six sessions. Consultations were very thorough. In the first part of 1991 however, only four of 22 inmates considered in need of psychiatric assessment and treatment had been transferred so that it might be obtained. Prompter transfers should be made possible and delays in obtaining places should be monitored.

Injuries and self-inflicted harm
6.12   Injuries to inmates should be recorded on a Form F213; we did not find any F213s which had been raised but could not believe that no injuries had been sustained. We therefore recommend that all injuries are recorded in the proper way.

6.13   Instances of self-inflicted harm should be recorded on a Form F220; only four such forms had been raised in 1990 and 1991 (to the date of the inspection). The reason for this very low total is that many

71

instances of self-inflicted harm are classified as
'gestures' only and therefore not recorded. This is not
acceptable. All instances of self-harm should be
recorded as such and discussed by the SPMG.

Sexually-transmitted diseases

6.14   A physician in Genito-Urinary medicine visited
as required but the service provided appeared to be
limited to inmates who were HIV positive or had penile
warts. We recommend a better genito-urinary service
should be developed with a clear statement of aims.

Section B   Special Features

Lifers

6.15   At the time of the inspection, 36 inmates were
serving indeterminate sentences, some of whom were in
Category A. The institution had an agreed maximum of 40
lifers but it was thought it might be able to take up to
45 if necessary.

6.16   Aylesbury was a Lifer Centre for young offenders
serving indeterminate sentences. This meant it was the
first allocation after conviction for young lifers and
one where they could normally expect to remain, under
assessment, until their transfer to an adult prison on
reaching 21 years of age.

6.17   Most of the institution's lifer population was
concentrated in F and G Wings. A small number were,
however, allocated to A, B and C Wings. Staff had mixed
views about whether a Lifer Unit would be an advantage
but there were currently no plans to set one up.
Allocation of lifers to employment was the same as for
non-lifers via the Labour Board and lifers could apply
(except those in Category A) for any job in the prison.

6.18   All inmates at Aylesbury were allocated a Personal Officer (see also 5.06). Personal Officers prepared reports for, and attended, both Sentence Planning Review Boards (SPRBs) and Long Term Review Boards (LTRBs). All trainees attended a SPRB every six months; those serving ten years or more and lifers additionally attended two LTRBs in their first year and subsequently one each year thereafter. We were satisfied that lifers were being properly assessed and reviewed. Psychiatric and psychological support was generally satisfactory and there were lifer groups looking at both lifer-specific matters (like the tariff) and topics of more general interest - the latter relied heavily on outside speakers. A successful 'Lifer Day' had been held for lifers and their families.

CHAPTER SEVEN

CONCLUSIONS

7.01   With Castington and Swinfen Hall, Aylesbury is designated to hold those trainees serving the longest sentences, including life sentences, and receives the more difficult trainees. It is generally regarded, and often referred to, as the 'Dispersal Prison' for the Young Offender system.

7.02   A population which combines the features of youth, violent offending and lengthy sentences will always present challenges to prison staff. Trainees at Aylesbury frequently provide just such a challenge to the good order and discipline of the establishment. The problem for the Governor lies in deciding the appropriate level of response that is required to change and control negative behaviour. The aim is always to provide an environment which is both safe and creative. The recent history of Aylesbury suggests that it has moved through various stages of control to a point where the staff are now in full control. Management systems are in place and the Establishment is ready to move forward. However, there are a number of developments which need to occur first.

7.03   In an unpublished part of this report we have listed a number of security measures that must be taken if the establishment is to hold the highest security categories.

7.04   Aylesbury's place within the system must be clarified and supported. The issues relating to holding Category A trainees are set out in the Preface. The role of the proposed medical centre is an important part of this equation. Alternative establishments should be identified that would enable some trainees to be allocated closer to their homes as well as providing another venue for the more troublesome. A review needs to be carried out of the sentence length criteria being operated in various establishments, these must overlap so that the system as a whole can respond with flexibility.

7.05   At a local level, the central need is to introduce a broader concept of training supported by a range of activities. Opportunities need to be created for more practical work. The relevance of some trade training and the content of some of the courses should be reviewed. The future of the PSIF workshop needs to be considered against alternative options, a charity workshop for example.

7.06   Facilities and opportunities for activities need to be improved and increased. Periods of association are restricted by the space available as much as by staffing. The match between the work to be undertaken by the staff and their availability needs to become much closer. This will enable the Governor to address such issues as the spread of meal times, the availability of visits, the frequency and duration of association and outside activities.

7.07   The average net operating cost per inmate per week for 1989/90 was £400. At Castington it was £390 and Swinfen Hall £560. The average for all YO closed establishments was £346. Given the very difficult nature of the population we considered Aylesbury provided good value for money.

7.08   We have identified a number of areas where improvements should be made. They include food,

workshops, association, library and visits. We
recognise that Governor and staff are aware of them. We
found Aylesbury to be a problematic establishment that
was well managed and well supported by its staff.

CHAPTER EIGHT

RECOMMENDATIONS

FOR ACTION BY THE DIRECTOR GENERAL
We recommend that:-

8.1   The role of Aylesbury within the young offender estate should be clearly defined. (3.04)

8.2   A Medical Centre should be provided as a matter of urgency (subject to a decision on the institution's role). (6.07)

8.3   Category A inmates should not be held in Aylesbury until perimeter security is improved to an appropriate standard. (1.17)

8.4   The planned start of work on the new Gate complex should be brought forward. (1.16)

8.5   The redevelopment programme should include provision for a Visitors' Centre. (5.01)

8.6   Further consideration should be given to the problems facing staff posted to Aylesbury from other parts of the country. (1.27 and 2.32)

8.7   Vacancies at Senior Officer level should be filled by substantive promotions. (2.33)

8.8   Unless a regular supply of good-quality work can be made available, the PSIF workshop should be replaced by additional VT and CIT courses. (4.18)

8.9   PSIF should issue guidance on the washing of soiled
      and foul linen.   (4.20)

8.10 Inmates, particularly if there are any in Category
      A, should be transferred promptly to adult prisons
      on reaching 21 years of age.   (5.19)

8.11 The General Practice to which the part-time Medical
      Officer belongs should be invited to provide a
      service in the following areas: physiotherapy,
      minor operations and chiropody and the
      establishment funded accordingly.   (6.02)

8.12 Inmates needing psychiatric treatment should be
      transferred quickly to where it is available and
      any delays in placements should be monitored.
      (6.11)

8.13 The system of self-medication at Aylesbury should
      be considered for wider application in the Prison
      Service.   (6.08)

8.14 The need for so many patients to be sent to local
      hospitals should be examined.   (6.05)

FOR ACTION BY THE GOVERNOR

We recommend that:-

Maintenance

8.15 The Small Repairs System be used more widely and effectively. (1.14)

Security

8.16 - 8.21   Recommendations made in Secretary of State's report but not for publication.

Health and Safety

8.22 Safe Methods of Working documents should be completed. (1.19)

8.23 The Health and Safety Policy and Statement of Arrangements should be amplified and clarified. (1.19)

8.24 Safety Audits should be programmed and brought up-to-date. (1.19)

8.25 Work to satisfy the COSHH regulations should be brought up-to-date. (1.19)

8.26 All cold rooms should have internal lights and labels on door release catches. (1.20)

8.27 The victualling cold store should be fitted with an alarm, insulated door and door catch release. (1.20)

Fire precautions

8.28 The duties of the Fire Officer should be reviewed and appropriate time allocated for their satisfactory completion. (1.22)

8.29 All fire exit routes should be clearly marked.
     (1.23)

Facilities for people with disabilities
8.30 Facilities for the disabled should be surveyed
     annually as part of the Health and Safety Audit and
     appropriate provision made.   (1.24)

Board of Visitors
8.31 The Board of Visitors should have its own office,
     with a desk and telephone.   (1.26)

8.32 Reports by Board members on visits should be typed
     in the establishment.   (1.26)

Meetings
8.33 The system of local orders and notices to staff
     should be clarified.   (2.23)

8.34 Consideration should be given to setting-up the
     proposed Community Relations Group.   (2.22)

Management Services
8.35 The staffing of the Management Services Department
     should be the subject of a resource review.   (2.08)

8.36 Administrative assistance should be provided for
     the Education and Probation Departments.   (2.08,
     4.22 and 5.12)

8.37 The work of the Finance Committee should be
     reviewed.   (2.19)

Staff facilities
8.38 More showers for staff should be provided.   (2.27)

Race Relations

8.39 The under-representation of ethnic minorities on the CIT Painting and Decorating Course should be investigated by the Chairman of the Race Relations Management Group. (3.10)

8.40 The over-representation of inmates from ethnic minorities on minor reports should be investigated by the Chairman of the Race Relations Management Group. (3.10)

Reception

8.41 The Reception Unit should be refurbished and redecorated. (3.14)

Induction and information to inmates

8.42 The Induction Unit should be redecorated. (3.15)

8.43 At an appropriate stage during redevelopment, the Unit should be sited in larger accommodation. (3.15)

Inmate accommodation

8.44 The standard of cleanliness in communal and residential areas should be significantly improved. (3.24)

8.45 The refurbishment of F and G Wings should be pressed ahead quickly. (3.23)

Inmate facilities

8.46 Association areas should be provided in or near the wings. (3.27)

8.47 Water boilers should be provided in each wing. (3.28)

8.48 Hot cupboards in wing serveries should be used properly. (3.28)

8.49 The servery and wash-up area in F and G Wings should be kept clean. (3.28)

Segregation and the Segregation Unit

8.50 The staffing of the Segregation Unit should be reviewed. (3.38)

Adjudications

8.51 The Governor should review the local procedure for reporting offences. (3.41)

8.52 Adjudication records (Forms F256) should be subject to regular, scrutiny by the Governor. (3.41)

8.53 There should be regular meetings of adjudicating officers to ensure consistency of practice. (3.41)

Association and exercise

8.54 Full periods of association should be provided for all inmates each evening and during the day at weekends. (4.02)

8.55 Inmates should be offered the opportunity of one hour's exercise each day in the fresh air. (3.05(a) and 4.03)

Meal times

8.56 The mid-day and evening meals should be served substantially later in the day. (4.04)

Shop

8.57 The Shop should be thoroughly redecorated and better laid out. (4.08)

8.58 A larger range of stock should be carried including more ethnic minority and vegan items. (4.08)

8.59 Consideration should be given to partially civilianising the manning of the Shop. (4.08)

8.60 Consideration should be given to transferring pay calculation work from Shop staff to administrative staff. (4.08)

Clothing and Kit

8.61 A personal kit system should be introduced. (4.10)

8.62 Arrangements should be made to ensure that kit is properly controlled by staff. (4.09)

Catering

8.63 Cockroach infestation of the kitchen should be eradicated. (4.13)

8.64 Consideration should be given to the introduction of the Caterbase NVQ for inmates working in the kitchen. (4.11)

8.65 The quality of the meals served to inmates should be improved. (4.12)

8.66 Cleanliness in the kitchen should be improved. (4.13)

8.67 The inmate changing areas should be refurbished. (4.12)

8.68 The arrangements for the prevention of cross-contamination of different foods should be improved and particularly in relation to the fridge in the vegetable area and the meat preparation area. (4.13)

Farms and gardens

8.69 Higher priority should be afforded to improving the institution's garden areas, particularly where these are a potential threat to security. (4.21)

Education

8.70 Evening classes should be offered on four evenings each week during the teaching year and arrangements made for inmates from F and G Wings to attend on two of these. (4.23)

Vocational Training Courses

8.71 Consideration should be given to introducing at least one new VTC (see also 8.8). (4.27)

8.72 The Braille shop should be better equipped. (4.27)

Construction Industry Training Courses

8.73 The attendance and exam pass rates for the Painting and Decorating Course should be improved. (4.28)

8.74 At least one additional CIT course should be introduced (see also 8.8). (4.29)

Library

8.75 A single central library should be established to serve the entire institution. (4.30)

Physical Education

8.76 The showers in the gymnasium should be refurbished. (4.32)

8.77 The swimming pool should be covered, heated and provided with changing and showering facilities. (4.33)

8.78 Redevelopment should include the provision of a purpose-built sports hall. (4.33)

Religious activities

8.79 A multi-faith room should be provided. (4.35)

Visits

8.80 The visiting facilities should be redecorated and easy chairs and tables provided. (5.02)

8.81 Weekend visiting times should be extended by at least half-an-hour to enable all visits to last two hours. (3.05(h) and 5.01)

8.82 Visits should be held every day of the week. (5.01)

8.83 There should be proper facilities for conducting closed visits. (3.44)

8.84 There should be a designated private area in which to search inmates before and after visits. (3.44)

Probation

8.85 The Governor should consider how the Senior Probation Officer might be more fully integrated in the management of the establishment. (5.09)

8.86 Offices for probation staff should be available in each wing. (5.10)

8.87 Staff training should be available to assist with helping adolescent sex offenders at Aylesbury. (5.11)

8.88 Progress towards fulfilling the requirements of Circular Instruction 40/1988 should continue. (5.10)

Psychology

8.89 Proper interviewing facilities should be available in the wings. (5.13)

8.90 There should be improved co-ordination of individual work with inmates. (5.15)

MEDICAL

Staffing

8.91 The Medical Officer should be encouraged to attend meetings of the Senior Management Group. (6.02)

Hospital

8.92 Unused hospital accommodation should be reallocated for other purposes. (6.04)

8.93 The treatment room should not be in the Pharmacy. (6.08)

8.94 Consideration should be given to fitting safety netting at first-floor level in the hospital. (6.04)

Dental services

8.95 Long-term inmates and lifers should have regular automatic check-ups. (6.09)

8.96 Visits by the Dental Officer should be identifiably recorded at the Gate. (6.09)

8.97 The Dental Officer should (on average) see more than six patients per session and the dental waiting list should be reduced. (6.09)

8.98 Three full sets of sterilisable handpieces should be provided by the Prison Medical Services. (6.10)

8.99 The ethyl chloride spray in the dental surgery should be removed and disposed of safely. (6.10)

Sexually-transmitted diseases

8.100   A more pro-active genito-urinary service should be developed with a clear statement of aims. (6.14)

Injuries and self-inflicted injuries

8.101   All injuries should be recorded on a Form F213. (6.12)

8.102   All known self-inflicted injuries should be recorded on a Form F220 and be discussed by the Suicide Prevention Management Group. (6.13)

BREAKDOWN OF POPULATION BY SENTENCE LENGTH (AS AT 9 JULY 1991)

Sentence length	Number of inmates	% of total population
Over 6 months, up to 18 months	1	0.5
Over 18 months, up to 3 years	15	6
Over 3 years, up to 4 years	52	21.5
Over 4 years, up to 10 years	137	56
Over 10 years, less than life	2	1
Life	36	15
	————	
TOTAL	243	

POLICY GROUP   CENTRAL MANAGEMENT TEAM

HEAD OF PSYCHOLOGICAL ——————— SENIOR PSYCHOLOGIST ——————— HIGHER PSYCHOLOGIST ┬— PSYCHOLOGIST
SERVICES   └— PSYCHOLOGICAL ASSISTANT

HEAD OF MANAGEMENT ——————┬— TRAINING P.O. · · · · · · · · · · STAFF CLERK
SERVICES   │
                         ├— E.O. (PERSONNEL & ——————— CASHIER, FINANCE, MANAGEMENT INFORMATION
                         │   FINANCE)   SYSTEMS, GOV'S SEC; ADMIN. STAFF FOR EDUCATION,
                         │   PROBATION, INDUSTRIES, SWITCHBOARD.
                         │
                         └— E.O. (DISCIPLINE & ——————— DISCIPLINE/PAROLE; VICTUALLING, PRISONERS
                                SUPPLIES)   MONIES/EARNINGS, STOREMEN P.A's; TYPISTS,
                                                       STORES.

                         · ┬ · · · · · · · · CIT INSTRUCTOR
HEAD OF WORKS —————————┬— P.O. (CONTRACTS) ———————————————————————— AUXILIARIES
SERVICES   │
                       ├— P.O. (E & M) ——————— STO's ———————┬— T.O's
                       │
                       └— P.O. (BUILDING) ——————— STO ——————————— INDUSTRIAL STAFF

                         ┌—————————————————————— CONSULTANT PSYCHIATRIST
[P/T M.O.]* ————————————— HOSPITAL S.O. ——————————————————————— HOSPITAL OFFICERS

                              *

                       ┌— CATERING S.O. ——————————————————————— CATERING OFFICERS
                       │
                       ├— P.O. (PEI) ——————— SO (PEI) ——————— PEI's
                       │
HEAD OF INMATE ————————┼— CHAPLAIN ——————————————————————— VISITING MINISTERS
   ACTIVITIES   │
(3rd in Charge)   ├——————————————————————— LIBRARY OFFICER
                       │   ┆
                       ├— EDUCATION OFFICER ——————— DEP. EDUCATION ┬— TEACHERS
                       │   OFFICER   └— VTC INSTRUCTORS
                       │
                       └— INDUSTRIAL MANAGER ——————┬— SO (LAUNDRY) ——————— LAUNDRY INSTRUCTOR
                                                   └——————————————————————— CIO's (EME)

                                    ┌— SO (PUN) ——————— OFFICERS
                              ┌— PO(A) ——— SO's (A) ——————— OFFICERS
                              │
                   G5 (RES 1) ┼— PO(B) ——————— SO's (B) ——————— OFFICERS
                              │
                              └— PO(C) ——————— SO's (C) ——————— OFFICERS

HEAD OF CUSTODY ————————— G5 (RES 2) ┬— PO(F) ——————— SO's (F) ——————— OFFICERS
(2nd in Charge)   │
                                     └— PO(G) ——————— SO's (G) ——————— OFFICERS
                                                                    └— INDUCTION OFFICERS

                   G5 (OPS) ┬— SECURITY PO · · · · SO's (ECR) ——————— OFFICERS
                           │
                           └— OPS PO ——————— SO's (Ops) ——————— OFFICERS

                   SENIOR PROBATION OFFICER ——————————————————————— WING PROBATION
                                                                    OFFICERS

· · · · Secondary Accountability/*Temporary Accountability(awaiting appointment of F/T M.C

EMPLOYMENT

Type of Work	*EMC	Average Number employed over previous 6 months	Scheduled Weekly Opening Hours	Average weekly hours closed over previous 6 months
1. E.M.E.	36	14	21.5	NIL
2. WORKS	12	6.6	21.5	NIL
3. LAUNDRY	14	15	21.5	1.12
4.				
5.				
6.				
TOTAL	62	35.6		

Vocational Training Courses	*EMC	Average Number employed over previous 6 months		CIT Course	*EMC	Number Employed
1. BRAILLE	18	12		1. P & D	12	5
2. CATERING	10	9		2.		
3. RADIO/TV	10	5		3.		
4. EDOS	10	5		4.		
5. ELECT/WIRE	10	8				

Other Work (Domestic, Gardens, Kitchen, etc.)

Type of Work				Number of Red Bands	
1. KITCHEN	13	11		* Wing Cleaners	30
2. DOMESTIC	54*	40		FDR	8
3. STORES	6	5		GENERAL CLEANER	6
4. C.S.V.	3	1		ESTATE PARTY	4
5. INDUCTION	6	4		ORDERLIES	6

Full time education. 45 + 15 Part-Time

No work Available (Give reasons). GARDEN PARTY (6) NO INSTRUCTOR

Remand and Trials choosing not to work. N.A.

Total population 240.5 over past 12 months

*Effective Minimum Complement

HM YOUNG OFFENDER INSTITUTION AYLESBURY

OUR POLICY ON RACE AND EQUAL OPPORTUNITIES

Here at Aylesbury we have an absolute commitment to a policy of racial and sexual equality and equal opportunity.

This policy is based on the three principles of fairness, mutual respect and sensitivity to legitimate needs. It applies equally to trainees, staff and to job applicants.

Fairness demands equality of access to facilities, absence of discrimination based on race, ethnic origin, religion or sex. Decision making is not to be based on prejudice or stereotypes.

Mutual respect demands that racially or sexually derogatory or otherwise offensive language is not used towards or about other people. Those in a position to exercise authority or power are not to abuse their position.

Sensitivity to legitimate needs recognises the fact that "treating everybody the same" does not always result in fairness or equality. This is because peoples' needs differ.

STATEMENT OF PURPOSE HMYOI AYLESBURY

TO HOLD AND CONTROL TRAINEES IN SAFE, SECURE AND HUMANE
CONDITIONS WHILST PROVIDING VARIED OPPORTUNITIES TO THEM ALL,
REGARDLESS OF ETHNIC ORIGIN, TO MOTIVATE THEM TO USE THEIR TIME
HERE CONSTRUCTIVELY AND TO AVOID CRIMINAL BEHAVIOUR NOW AND IN
THE FUTURE.

	0900–1000	1015–1115	1330–1430	1430–1530	1730–1830	1915–2015
MONDAY	LAUNDRY I F D R F & G CLNRS STORES	COMMUNITY PROJECT	KITCHEN CAT. COURSE R/BANDS	RADIO TV ELEC. WIRING E D O S A WING L/UPS	G Y M G C S E M PRISON WEIGHTS	ACTIVITIES P.E F & G
TUESDAY	LAUNDRY II	E M E GEN. CLEANERS W/UP	STAFF RECREATIONAL HOUR	ESTATE PARTY B WING L/UPS	FITNESS F & G OLYMPIC LIFTING	FITNESS MAIN PRISON
WEDNESDAY	F D R F & G CLNS	INDUCTION OCCUPATIONAL HEALTH REMEDIALS	CAT. 'A's 'E's EQUIP. CHECK	RADIO TV ELEC WIRING E D O S	COMMUNITY LEADERS POWERLIFTING GROUP	SPORTS AWARD
THURSDAY	BRAILLE INSIDE WORKS M P CLNS STORES GDNS PARTY	E M E GEN. CLNS W/UP	KITCHEN CATER. COURSE R/BANDS PITCH MARKING	ESTATE PARTY C WING L/UPS	VOLLEYBALL M PRISON WEIGHTS	SQUAD F & G WEIGHTS
FRIDAY	CAT. 'A's 'E's	INDUCTIONS OCCUPATIONAL HEALTH REMEDIALS	LAUNDRY I II DISCHARGES	F & G LOCK UPS	RECREATIONAL P. E. F & G F & G WEIGHTS	M A I N PRISON MAIN PRISON WEIGHTS
SATURDAY	MAIN PRISON F/G GYM ACTIVITIES	MAIN PRISON F/G GYM ACTIVITIES	SUMMER OUTDOOR WINTER INDOOR ACTIVITIES	OUTDOOR ACTIVITIES INTER-WING RUGBY		
SUNDAY	PUNS. RULES	FIELD PREP CAT. 'A's 'E's GYM CLEANING	SUMMER OUTDOOR WINTER INTER-WING	ACTIVITIES COMPETITIONS		

99

AYLESBURY YOI PE Programme

THE INSPECTION TEAM

The full inspection of Aylesbury Young Offender Institution was carried out by the following members of the Inspectorate:-

Judge S Tumim	HM Chief Inspector of Prisons
Mr D Brooke	Governor 1
Mr J J Courtney	Grade 7
Mr J Gallagher	Governor 4
Mr A French	Staff Officer
Mr S Ratcliffe	Buildings Inspector
Mr G Williams	Medical Inspector